Green As a Frog

written by **Molly Dingles**

illustrated by **Walter Velez**

dingles & company New Jersey

©2002 by Judith Mazzeo Zocchi

First printing

PUBLISHED BY dingles&company

P.O. Box 508 • Sea Girt, New Jersey • 08750
WEBSITE: www.dingles.com • E-MAIL: info@dingles.com

LIBRARY BINDING EDITION DISTRIBUTED BY **GUMDROP BOOKS**
P.O. Box 505 • Bethany, Missouri • 64424
(660) 425-7777

Library of Congress Catalog Card No.: 2002141513
ISBN: 1-891997-21-1

Printed in the United States of America

●

ART DIRECTED & DESIGNED BY Barbie Lambert

EDITED BY Andrea Curley / EDITORIAL ASSISTANT Allison Bolte

DEVELOPMENT TEAM

Kathleen P. Miller, Meredith Paril,
Leslie Greenley

For Vincent III

Molly Dingles

is the author of *Jinka Jinka Jelly Bean* and *Little Lee Lee's Birthday Bang*. As Judy Zocchi, she has written the *Paulie & Sasha* series. She is a writer and lyricist who holds a bachelor's degree in fine arts/theater from Mount Saint Mary's College and a master's degree in educational theater from New York University. She lives in Manasquan, New Jersey, with her husband, David.

Walter Velez

was born in New York. He attended the High School of Art and Design and later the School of Visual Arts. He has done illustration work for many major book and gaming companies. He is known for the popular series *Thieves World* as well as the *Myth* series for Ace Books. He has also produced trading cards for *Goosebumps* and *Dune*. In addition, Walter has illustrated several *Star Wars* books for Random House. He lives in Queens, New York, with his wife, Kriti, and daughter, Kassandra.

The **Community of Color** series is more than just a series of books about colors. The series demonstrates how individual people, places, and things combine to form a community. It allows children to view the world in segments and then experience the wonderment and value of the community as a whole.

Green floppy ferns

Green moss on the ground

Green **leaping frog**

Green grass can be found.

Green squirming snake

Green bugs in a bunch

Green gliding moth

Green mango for lunch.

Green twisted vines

Green parrot in flight

Green X on the map

Green tent for the night.

The color Green is all around.

ABOUT COLOR

Use the Community of Color series to teach your child to identify the most basic colors and to help him or her relate these colors to objects in the real world. ASK:

- What color is this book about?
- Can you name all the green things in this jungle scene?
- How many green bugs can you find?
- What green fruit is in this picture?

ABOUT COMMUNITY

Use the Community of Color series to teach your child how he or she is an important part of the community. EXPLAIN TO YOUR CHILD WHAT A COMMUNITY IS:

- A community is a place where people live, work, and play together.
- Your family is a community.
- Your school is a community.
- Your neighborhood is a community.
- The world is one big community.

Everyone plays an important part in making a community work - moms, dads, boys, girls, police officers, firefighters, teachers, mail carriers, garbage collectors, store clerks, and even animals are all important parts of a community. USE THESE QUESTIONS TO FURTHER THE CONVERSATION:

- How are the people in this jungle interacting with one another?
- How are the people different from one another? How are they the same?
- What do they have in common?
- How is the community you see in this book like your community? How is it different?
- Describe your community.

ABOUT FEELINGS

Colors can describe as well as evoke different emotions. Encourage your child to describe the feelings that the color green inspires. ASK:

- How does the color green make you feel?
- Name your favorite green thing in this book. Why is it your favorite?
- Name your favorite green thing at home. Why is it your favorite?
- Can you tell how the people in the picture feel by looking at their faces?
  Do you ever feel the same way? When? Why?

TRY SOMETHING NEW . . . Lend a hand! Plant a tree with green leaves at your school for the community to enjoy (but get permission before you do).